MEDIEVAL
SECRETS
&
SCANDALS

IMPORTANT DATES

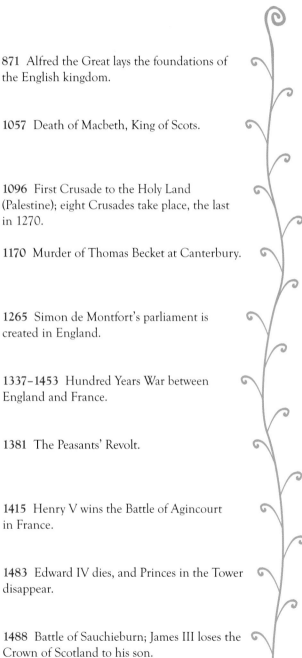

871 Alfred the Great lays the foundations of the English kingdom.

1016 Death of Ethelred II, the 'Unready'.

1057 Death of Macbeth, King of Scots.

1066 The Normans invade Anglo-Saxon England.

1096 First Crusade to the Holy Land (Palestine); eight Crusades take place, the last in 1270.

1139 Civil war in England; it ends when Henry II becomes king in 1154.

1170 Murder of Thomas Becket at Canterbury.

1215 Magna Carta is sealed by King John.

1265 Simon de Montfort's parliament is created in England.

1314 Battle of Bannockburn; the Scots, led by Robert Bruce, defeat the English.

1337–1453 Hundred Years War between England and France.

1348 The Black Death.

1381 The Peasants' Revolt.

1399 Henry Bolingbroke overthrows Richard II.

1415 Henry V wins the Battle of Agincourt in France.

1455 Wars of the Roses begin in England.

1483 Edward IV dies, and Princes in the Tower disappear.

1485 Battle of Bosworth; Henry VII becomes the first Tudor King of England.

1488 Battle of Sauchieburn; James III loses the Crown of Scotland to his son.

1492 Columbus sails to America and a new world is opened up.

➤➤ Court ladies watch jousting knights, from a 14th-century manuscript.

INTRODUCTION

The Middle Ages, or medieval period, spans the centuries from the 400s to the 1500s. In Britain, visible legacies are castles and cathedrals, but remembered from history and legends are kings and queens, and fabled heroes such as Robin Hood. Power lay with the Court and the Church, but rumour and gossip rippled around water-well and market place, for that was how news spread. Around the kings, whose powers were as many as their human frailties, murder, mischief and muck-raking simmered. Here are whispers of old passions and quarrels: murderous kings and queens, scheming lords and ladies, brutal barons and worldly clerics, witchcraft and magic. Many secrets and scandals were concealed behind the rich tapestries of the medieval pageant.

SAXON AND NORMAN SCANDALS

Medieval courts were seldom peaceful, for a hasty quarrel could spark years of blood-feud and murder. Violence was almost casual, even though there were laws to control it in Anglo-Saxon England – the payment of 'wergild' was compensation for a death. To defy royal law was risky, but sometimes it was the king who suffered. English king Edmund the Elder was murdered in 946 by Leofa, an outlaw who turned up at a Gloucestershire party, possibly to argue his case. Edmund tried to throw him out and was knifed.

More usually kings fell victim to ambitious relatives. In 978 King Edward, only 16, was murdered at Corfe, almost certainly by his stepmother Aelfthryth. She allegedly gave him poison, stabbed him (or had him killed) and installed her son Ethelred as king. Edward's 'martyred' bones were kept at Shaftesbury Abbey until the 1500s when they disappeared. They were rediscovered in 1931, and after some dispute ended up in the care of the Russian Orthodox Church.

DON'T TRUST THE GRASPER

Ethelred had disgraced himself as a baby, by peeing into the font at his baptism. A bad sign. Ethelred the 'unready' was more accurately 'unraed', Anglo-Saxon for ill-advised. His worst adviser was Edric

King Ethelred, unready and ill-advised.

Streona, known to contemporaries as 'Grasper': ambitious, tenacious and treacherous in equal measure. Edric and Ethelred paid off invading Vikings, and when bribes failed, ordered the St Brice's Day Massacre (1002) of Viking settlers in the 'Danelaw'. This provoked King Sweyn of Denmark to invade England, and Ethelred fled to Normandy. Edric clung on and,

Sweyn and the Danes land in England seeking vengeance.

after Ethelred's death in 1016, threw in his lot with the new English hope Edmund Ironside, only to desert him in battle and then (it was rumoured) murder him. In the most lurid version of events, Edric arranged for his son to hide in the pit beneath the royal privy. When Edmund sat above, he was stabbed from below. King Sweyn's son Cnut, now King of England, considered Edric's trustworthiness. Cnut had him killed within a year – a case of 'the biter bit', perhaps?

LADY GODIVA'S RIDE

This famous medieval shocker of a bareback ride through Coventry was first recounted by Roger of Wendover in the early 1200s. If it happened at all, it happened in 1043. Godiva (Godgifu) was the wife of Earl Leofric of Mercia. Angered by the killing of two tax-gatherers, Leofric upped the tax-burden, and his unhappy people appealed to Godiva. She argued with Leofric and, in exasperation, he challenged her to 'ride naked through Coventry if you're so concerned'. When she did, her flowing hair preserving her modesty, all the citizens shut their windows, except one – Peeping Tom, who was struck blind.

For an Anglo-Saxon noblewoman to appear naked is most unlikely; medieval women were normally covered up, including their hair and neck. In a public act of penitence, Godiva might have taken off her jewels, brooches and gold hair pins for her ride through Coventry, which was still only a big village rather than the city it later became.

SQUALID SONS OF CNUT

King Cnut, famous for bellowing at the incoming tide to demonstrate the limits of regal power to sycophantic courtiers, became a pious king with two impious sons. Harold I (Harefoot), who succeeded Cnut in 1035, was the son of the late king's mistress, Aelfgifu of Northampton. Cnut's wife Queen Emma (Ethelred's widow) had wanted her son Harthacnut to be king, but he was away in Denmark and Harold got in first. Harold banished Emma and had her son Alfred (brother of Edward the Confessor) blinded then shut away in a monastery. When Harold died in 1040, Harthacnut had his body dug up and thrown into the river. The new king was just as vile however, 'plundering the property of the citizens', and died unlamented in 1042 of a 'terrible convulsion' after binge-drinking at a wedding.

◄ The statue of Lady Godiva in Coventry.

WHO LIED FIRST?

With Cnut's sons gone, the Anglo-Saxon dynasty resumed with Edward the Confessor (1042–66). He did not look or act like a warrior king – he was very tall, very thin, very pale, and spent most of his time in prayer. Cajoled, or forced, to marry the daughter of Earl Godwin, the king was said to have refused conjugal relations. The union was, unsuprisingly, childless. With no heir, favourites to succeed Edward were Earl Godwin's son Earl Harold and the Norman Duke William, with Harold Hardrada of Norway an outside bet. William said he'd been promised the crown by Edward in 1051. Furthermore, in 1064 Harold had sworn not to oppose him. Harold argued that any 'promise' was made under duress, since he was William's prisoner at the time, and that Edward's deathbed wish in his favour superseded all others. Maybe neither was lying?

The sight of Halley's Comet at this time increased the sense of foreboding in England. Harold was

▲ The death of Harold, from the Bayeux Tapestry.

backed by most English nobles but not by his brother Tostig, who threw in with Hardrada. The Pope supported William's invasion of 1066, and the result was the Norman Conquest. Harold beat Hardrada and Tostig at Stamford Bridge on 25 September, but lost at Hastings on 14 October, his death yielding William the kingdom – though there are those who claim Harold II escaped death. Only the king's mistress Edith Swanneck could identify his mangled corpse, 'by secret marks'.

A LUCKY SHOT?

With Harold dead, the English nobility was stripped of land and power, and everyone grumbled. Rebels plotted, but uprisings faltered against Norman castles and mail-clad cavalry. Wanting no secrets, William ordered Domesday Book, to see what he had conquered. When the Conqueror died in 1087, his youngest son, Henry, could not have expected to become king without more than a little good fortune. One brother, Richard, was already dead from a hunting accident in the New Forest in 1075. Brother Robert ruled Normandy, and brother William Rufus became King of England. William was almost certainly gay, greedy and his ruddy complexion matched his hot Norman temper. He was money-grabbing and unloved, and his court was louche, all long hair and pointed shoes.

THE ROYAL TOUCH

Edward the Confessor was thought to be able to cure scrofula (the 'king's evil') and other ailments by the laying on of hands. The king was said to have cured a woman with a tumour from which 'the worms flowed out with the purulent matter'. Within a year she gave birth to twins!

◄ Edward the Confessor, a statue at Lichfield Cathedral.

CHOKING ON HIS WORDS

Earl Godwin was the power in England during most of Edward the Confessor's reign. Godwin's hopes that daughter Edith's marriage to the king would start a Godwin royal dynasty were dashed, and he did not live to see his son Harold become king, albeit briefly. One version of the devious Earl's death in 1053 describes him at dinner, protesting, 'may this morsel of bread choke me if I have been false' – following which he promptly collapsed.

In 1100 there came about a remarkable 'coincidence': while hunting in his father's New Forest, William Rufus was shot and killed by a stray arrow. Brother Henry moved fast, seizing the royal treasure from Winchester, and was crowned three days after the shooting. To avoid any altercation, he had brother Robert safely locked up – perfectly normal royal behaviour for the time.

◄ William II (Rufus): accident victim, or was he murdered?

▼ Battle of Hastings.

SCOTS VS ENGLISH

▲ Edward I, 'Hammer of the Scots'.

SCANDALOUS INTERFERENCE

It was no secret that England's Edward I (1239–1307) wanted to control Scotland and he now made a move. From thirteen claimants, he chose a puppet-ruler in John Balliol (1292–96). Most Scots were scandalised. When the hapless Balliol tried to rebel, he was crushed and the royal arms stripped from his tunic, so the Scots jeered 'toom tabard' (empty coat). Edward I hammered Scottish pride further by removing the sacred Stone of Destiny, also known as the Stone of Scone, and ignored the Pope's call for an English withdrawal from Scotland.

◄ William Wallace on his monument, erected at Dryburgh in 1814.

S cots and English lived in a near-permanent state of enmity, with secret treaties, broken promises and cross-border raids interspersed with diplomatic marriages to patch things up. Things went badly wrong for the Scots after the reign of Alexander III (1246–86). After Alexander's queen and only son both died in 1275, he remarried, but while riding to visit his new bride one stormy night, his horse tumbled him over a cliff to his death. Next in line was his grandchild Margaret (the 'Maid of Norway'). Motherless from birth, the poor child, only 3, died in Orkney after her storm-tossed voyage from Scandinavia.

◄ The Stone of Destiny rested beneath the coronation chair in Westminster Abbey until its return to Scotland in 1996.

BRUCE AND SON

Robert the Bruce's ancestry on his father's side was Norman. The king was 50 when his only son, David, was born in 1324. At 3, the child was married to Joanna, sister of Edward III of England. Bruce died in 1329, and his son David II's ups and downs over a reign of forty-one years included eleven years' captivity in England.

To end such scandalous interference, the Scots were led by William Wallace, Robert the Bruce and John Comyn (Balliol's nephew). Bruce and Comyn liked neither Wallace nor each other. Wallace was eventually betrayed (by whom is disputed), and taken to London for execution in 1305. Bruce tried to patch up his feud with Comyn, but Comyn leaked details to the English, who almost surprised and captured Bruce. When the two met in Greyfriars Church in Dumfries, Bruce killed Comyn.

FAMILY FORTUNES

Edward I regarded Bruce's family as fair game. He imprisoned Bruce's wife and daughter, and beheaded three brothers and a brother-in-law. Bruce's sister Mary was caged for 4 years in a 'chamber hung from the walls' of Roxburgh Castle, until moved to make sure she was still a usable hostage. Bruce took to the hills, learning perseverance – by watching a spider, if the tale is to be believed. When Edward I died in 1307, Bruce had already proclaimed himself King of Scotland.

THE LOST STONE

Bruce now demanded the return of the Stone of Destiny. The English refused. Legend had it that this sandstone block had been brought to Scotland by the daughter of an Egyptian pharaoh. At the time of Bruce's demand it reposed beneath the coronation chair in Westminster Abbey, and there it remained until 1996.

STARVED TO DEATH

Starving a prisoner to death was not an unusual medieval occurrence. During David II's reign (1329–71), Douglas of Liddesdale seized his enemy Sir James Ramsay, locked him up in Hermitage Castle and forgot about him. William Bullock, an official arrested for treason, was also starved to death at Lochindorb Castle in Moray.

▲ Hermitage Castle, Roxburghshire, haunted by its sinister history.

ROYAL SCANDALS

The medieval court was riven by family disputes, and occasionally darkened by tragic accidents with scandalous overtones. In 1120, Henry I was sailing from Normandy to England. His son William was following on a second vessel, the *White Ship*, along with Richard and Matilda, two of the king's numerous illegitimate children. William was Henry I's only legitimate male heir. The noble passengers were in high spirits, with drinks flowing freely, and so they challenged the oarsmen to overtake the king's ship pulling out of harbour. The *White Ship* struck a submerged rock and the cries of the drowning were mistaken for revelry. Only two sailors struggled ashore. For a king to lose his male heir was a disaster. Henry 'never smiled again'.

WARRING MATILDA

Henry I had married his daughter Matilda to the Holy Roman Emperor in 1114. It was no secret that after the *White Ship* disaster, he pinned all his hopes on her. Her second marriage to Geoffrey of Anjou had produced two sons, Henry and Geoffrey, but Matilda was still the strongest claimant for the throne. However, when Henry I died in 1135, the notion of a female monarch was too much for his barons, and enough of them backed Matilda's cousin Stephen of Blois to generate a civil war that persisted until 1154. Matilda, more German than English in her ways, did not endear herself to the people, confiscating lands and mouthing abuse when petitioners came to complain. Her adventures during

▼ The wrecking of the *White Ship*.

▲ Henry I died in 1135 after eating lampreys. He had gone against his doctor's advice since the fish always upset him.

MATILDA'S MARRIAGES

Matilda was betrothed, aged 7, to the German monarch Henry V, thirty years her senior, and she married him in 1114, aged 12. Henry became Holy Roman Emperor and had her trained in all things German. When he died in 1125, Matilda's father Henry I ordered her back, to marry Geoffrey of Anjou who, at 15, was 10 years Matilda's junior. Their son became Henry II.

the civil war included escaping from Oxford across the snow, clad in white. Stephen just about won the war, but Matilda saw her son become king, as Henry II. On her deathbed in 1167 she became a nun.

THE BECKET MURDER

Henry II, England's king from 1154, had a blend of charm and rage attributed by his foes to an ancestral union with the Devil. He had a formidable wife, Eleanor of Aquitaine, and a formidable friend in churchman Thomas Becket. Becket stuck up for Church rights, and was not afraid to call a baron a pimp for arranging mistresses for the royal bed. The friendship was soured, however, by violent disagreements; Becket was for a while exiled, returning only to infuriate Henry further by scolding him for being crowned by inferior prelates, instead of by Becket. 'Will no man rid me of this turbulent priest?' Henry shouted to no one in particular. In December 1170, four knights sailed

▲ The murder of Thomas Becket in 1170.

from Normandy to England, rode to Canterbury, and butchered Becket in his cathedral. The murder shocked Christendom, and Henry let himself be scourged by monks as public penance. Becket's shrine in Canterbury became a magnet for pilgrims.

▲ King Richard I, The Lionheart (1157–99).

GOOD KING RICHARD?

Henry II had two sons, Richard and John, who became kings of England. Richard I was very tall, handsome and soldierly, but was hardly ever in the country – he was either crusading to the Holy Land or battling in France. Despite his glamour, unflattering stories circulated: that he had gone to bed with King Philip of France (a family arch-enemy); that he had ordered a massacre of Jews when Jewish leaders turned up for his coronation; that he had joked that, if he could find a buyer, he would sell London. On the way back from Crusade in 1192 Richard was captured by Leopold of Austria – doubly unlucky since the English regarded Austrians as 'more like wild beasts than men'. Richard hid in the kitchen, but forgot to remove his 'bling' (a ring far too showy for any servant). He was held hostage in Durnstein Castle until, as the legend goes, the loyal minstrel Blondel found him, the ransom was paid and Richard freed. Philip of France warned Prince John, who had been free from brotherly restraint in England, 'look to yourself, the Devil is loose'.

BAD KING JOHN?

After Richard I died in France in 1199, killed by a crossbow, brother John misruled until 1216. Was John really the scandalously bad king of Hollywood Robin Hood films? True, he behaved badly: he made fun of the beards of Irish chieftains; he giggled and dropped a ceremonial lance while being invested Duke of Normandy. Worse, in 1203 he drunkenly murdered his nephew Prince Arthur and had his body thrown into the River Seine. His wife Isabella detested him, and he her, claiming she was depraved. John was a blasphemer and a lecher, shocking foreign rulers who heard reports of his pursuit of barons' wives. One baron

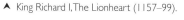

substituted a whore when the king demanded his wife; John enjoyed the night so much that the next day he complimented the baron on his marital good fortune.

For John, having to put his seal to Magna Carta, the 'great charter' between king and barons in 1215 that placed restraints on his power as monarch, was bad enough. Losing the Crown jewels in the Wash was the final disgrace. While the king was travelling in East Anglia in the autumn of 1216, the royal baggage train foundered in treacherous tidal quicksand. What was lost will never be known – the king especially lamented the loss of his religious relics. Sick with dysentery, he died after eating peaches to cheer himself up. There were those who whispered that 'John Lackland' had been poisoned – and good riddance.

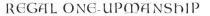

REGAL ONE-UPMANSHIP

Few ordinary people saw the king close up – most caught only a glimpse as he rode around his kingdom, being entertained by barons hoping to improve, or save, their reputations. Kings competed to outdo one another, and Henry III boasted Europe's finest menagerie: the Tower of London had a lion, three leopards, a bear and a camel, and the first elephant in England – at least since Roman times.

REVOLTING REMEDIES

For hard-riding knights suffering from saddle-sores and, worse, anal fistulas, Doctor John Arderne in 1376 recommended balms made from mutton, pig fat and pigeon dung. A little mumbo-jumbo and a joke boosted patient confidence, he said – as did a fat fee. Arsenic powder for open wounds unfortunately ate into the bone, but he also recommended 'the blood of love' – ideally a virgin's blood, but the doctor sold a red powder that did just as well.

◄◄ Crusaders on their way to the Holy Land. Opportunism and greed often diverted them from their purposes.

◄ King John agrees to Magna Carta in 1215. The quill pen is an artistic anachronism: the king would have affixed a seal to the document.

Church and Crime

Religious relics, like those King John lost in the Wash, were pillars of the medieval Church, in an age when faith and superstition had an almost equal hold. Kings valued their personal collections – Edward III reputedly paid 100 shillings for the 'undershirt' of St Peter. There was a brisk trade in 'genuine' relics – the feather from an angel's wing, or a bit of sailcloth from St Peter's fishing boat. Westminster Abbey had the shrine of Saint Edward the Confessor, the Virgin Mary's veil, the blade bone of St Benedict, a finger of St Alphage, half the jaw of St Anastasia, and a vial of Christ's blood. Reformers questioned the morality of the commercial trade in relics, and the sale of the forgiveness of sins (people could buy pardons). There were scandals, but to challenge the authority of the Church was dangerous – the Cathar heretics in France were butchered in a crusade in the 1200s. England, spared such horrors,

▼ The capture of Montségur Castle in France, where over 200 Cathars were burned alive during the 13th-century Cathar Crusade.

▲ St Peter, Christ's disciple and first bishop of Rome; from a medieval stained-glass window.

saw churches shut for six years after King John refused to accept the Pope's choice of Archbishop of Canterbury. No baptisms, weddings or funerals took place, except in parishioners' homes or churchyards. After John was excommunicated, he gave in – not even a king dared risk his soul's damnation.

The Duchess and the Witch

Even more risky than heresy was sorcery. Beautiful Eleanor Cobham became the mistress of the Duke of Gloucester, younger brother of Henry V.

A war hero wounded at Agincourt (1415), ending his marriage to wed Eleanor dented the Duke's reputation. Worse, his new Duchess was accused of seeing a witch. Eleanor said she had consulted Margery Jourdemayne for advice on getting pregnant, but enemies scented a conspiracy: the king, Henry VI, was a child still in Gloucester's care, only too vulnerable to some magical sickness. Arrests of Eleanor's confidantes were made in the summer of 1441. Thomas Southwell, a scholar, died in the Tower of London. Clerk Roger Bolingbroke was hanged, drawn and quartered. Margery Jourdemayne was burned at the stake. Eleanor was luckier; after public penance, and divorce, she was locked up until her death at Beaumaris Castle in Wales in 1452.

CONSPICUOUS CONSUMPTION

While the nobility were plotting, philandering or profiteering, the poor scraped by, and tried to keep out of trouble with the lord of the manor whose word was law. The local priest scared them with talk of devils and hellfire, but the here and now had enough nastiness: days of desperately hard work, disease and dirt. The medieval nose barely wrinkled at the rich mix of stinks from rubbish pits, privies, horses and pigs, and chamber pots emptied from windows. While the poor lived on pottage (a thick soup made from whatever ended up in the pot), the most righteous, the lord bishops, could feast like princes.

AN EPISCOPAL FEAST

In 1465, when George Neville was enthroned as Archbishop of York, 28 lords, 59 knights and 7 bishops were among more than 2,000 guests and servants who ate 4,000 pigeons, 2,000 chickens, 4,000 wild duck, 500 partridges, 800 swans and herons, 113 oxen, 1,000 sheep, 2,000 pigs and 500 deer. To wash down all this meat, plus jellies, pastries, custards and cakes, they drank 300 tuns of ale and 100 tuns of wine (a tun was 200–250 gallons).

CLERICAL SCANDALS

Poor 'clerks' or priests would marry, baptise or bury for a few pennies. The scholarly Roger Bacon sneered at their ignorance, suggesting many country parsons recited services without a clue as to the words' meaning. Though the Church endorsed celibacy, some priests had wives or mistresses. In 1373, 10 priests in Norwich were caught having relationships: for keeping two women, one was fined 5 shillings, while the priest at Dawlish in Devon kept his 'concubine' even after being 'corrected'. Other priestly failings included using churches as farmyards and breweries. Yet when disaster struck, in the Black Death of 1348, many clerks died serving their stricken communities.

➤ A Black Death victim awaits his fate.

Nuns lived more easy-going lives than monks, for female religious houses (nunneries) often served as retirement retreats, voluntary or enforced, for noblewomen. Some abbesses allowed too much jollity; the Prioress of Stamford confessed to the Bishop of Lincoln that one of her nuns had run off to Newcastle with a harp player. Critics said nuns took pet rabbits and dogs to church, and brazenly wore fine clothes and jewellery, like the Prioress in Chaucer's *Canterbury Tales* who sported a coral trinket on her arm, gaudy beads and a gold brooch.

TORTURE CHAMBERS

When crimes were committed, there was little concern for prisoner welfare. Punishments were brisk and often fatal – even a day in the stocks could leave the victim seriously wounded by missiles flung by unsympathetic onlookers. Captives not hanged or beheaded might face tortures of often grotesque unpleasantness. At Chillingham Castle in Northumberland, chained prisoners had an open-sided cage containing a starved rat fastened to their stomach. What went on inside castle dungeons was best not thought about: boiling pots, eye-gougers, barrels with spikes on the inside, red-hot branding irons. Some prisoners were simply thrown into a tiny cell, or 'oubliette', and forgotten; private miseries rarely becoming public scandals.

TRANSPORT SCANDALS

There were many public complaints about the country's roads, which in winter were often impassable and where robbers 'and other malefactors' lay in wait. Few real-life outlaws were Robin Hoods, and the poor were robbed as freely as the rich, so pilgrims rode together for safety and merchants hired armed guards. Edward I ordered that highways between market towns be cleared of 'woods, hedges and ditches ... wherein a man may lurk to do hurt'. The weary traveller who made it safely to an inn was warned to beware of thieves and fleas – he must wash and rub his legs vigorously before bed, to brush off the previous guest's fleas. Lice and bed bugs were inescapable.

◀ Iron maiden, a medieval torture device.

▼ Characters from Geoffrey Chaucer's *Canterbury Tales*, including the Prioress.

STUDENT RIOTS

To help constables, sheriffs and other law officers keep the king's peace, there was a nightly curfew. By this time fires had to be put out or made safe, and taverns had to evict the last drinkers – in 1309 Edward II decreed no tavern was to sell wine or beer after curfew. Fencing schools, like that run by 'Roger the Skirmisher', enticed respectable youths 'to the injury of their characters', so were shut down. Students were a nuisance, with frequent brawls in the university towns of Oxford and Cambridge, and in 1298 scandalous allegations of 'loose women' in colleges were made. After 'snappish words' in a tavern provoked a 'town and gown' battle in Oxford, houses were ransacked and books flung into the street. Student offences were legion: drinking, shooting bows, visiting brothels, keeping ferrets, hawks and hunting dogs, and (less heinous) walking on the grass.

London Bridge was new in 1176 but in 1282 five of the bridge's arches collapsed into the Thames – a scandal remembered in the rhyme 'London Bridge is falling down'. Elsewhere many bridges were crumbling, with reports of wagons and horses falling into rivers and people drowning. Those paid to maintain roads and bridges were too often found wanting, lining their pockets with toll-money.

THE JUDGE FOUND OUT

In 1388 Judge Robert Tresham was arrested in Westminster having been found 'dressed like a beggar, hiding under a table'. Tresham was accused of necromancy and treason, for on his body were 'charms and signs', including the head of a demon. At his inevitable execution, Tresham refused to climb the ladder to the scaffold – until whipped – declaring he could not be hanged as he was immortal. He was hanged naked and his throat cut to make sure.

MAGIC AND MURDER

Most people in the Middle Ages were superstitious as well as religious. They believed in the supernatural, and in magic and witchcraft, for good or evil. From Anglo-Saxon times, many people wore charms and muttered spells to protect themselves from accidents, disease, wild beasts or spirits of the unknown world – elves, sprites, goblins, fairies. Folk memories of ancient pre-Christian traditions and pagan gods were no doubt evoked by mysterious monuments such as standing stones, dolmens and long barrows. Such places were usually avoided, and associated with secret meetings of witches and demons.

THE ALCHEMISTS

Alchemists sought the 'philosopher's stone' that would turn lead into gold and the 'elixir' that would bring eternal life and youth. Roger Bacon (born c.1220) was interested in maths, optics and astronomy, and is said to have been the first in England to describe gunpowder – the 'devilish' explosive from Asia. Science was easily mistaken for magic, however, and Bacon was shut up in a Paris religious house for fourteen years after his work upset the authorities.

▼ A 15th-century depiction of the Devil.

▼ The Men-an-Tol standing stones near Penzance in Cornwall, renowned for curing many ailments by passing the sufferer through the hole. The stones were also seen as a charm against witchcraft or ill-wishing, and were used as a tool for augury or telling the future.

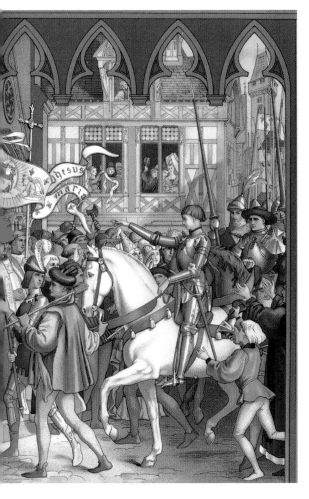

◀ Joan of Arc entering the besieged city of Orleans where she defeated the English and their French allies.

In Scotland, the 'witches of Forres', found roasting a wax effigy of King Duff, were burned to death in 968. In the early 1300s, after Pope Boniface VIII quarrelled with King Philip IV of France (mainly over taxation), he was posthumously accused of murder, magic and sodomy. Joan of Arc, the inspiration for French armies against the English, and a devoutly religious peasant girl, was burned as a witch in 1431. Anyone behaving oddly – the old, lonely, or the mentally disturbed – risked being seen as 'perverted by Satan' and accused of witchcraft: cohabiting with demons, riding at night with the pagan goddess Diana, causing sickness and death, killing cattle, even turning neighbours' milk sour. Yet full-scale witch-hunts were rare. They became more common after the Black Death of 1348.

THE REAL BLUEBEARD

Gilles de Rais (1405–40) fought alongside Joan of Arc against the English. High-profile and flamboyant, he developed a fatal interest in black magic, turning to serial murder; he was accused of kidnapping, torturing and killing hundreds of children. His sex-crimes inspired the later 'Bluebeard' story of Charles Perrault. Gilles de Rais and two accomplices were hanged, though a 1990s 'retrial' suggested he was framed.

GOOD AND BAD MAGIC

There was 'good magic', for healing wounds or ensuring safe childbirth, and charms for use against 'the fiend's temptation' or for curing a 'wit-sick' person. Useful tips abounded, such as giving a gossiping woman a radish to eat to stop her speaking ill of you the next day. People told stories of fabled wizards, such as Merlin, and gasped at magic tricks: fire-eating, conjuring and the spectacular special effects in medieval plays – religious in message but magical in performance.

To be accused of black magic was very dangerous for one's life, soul and reputation, however.

MAGICAL ACCUSATION

In 1382 Nicholas Freeman and his wife Cristina were accused of theft, after a neighbour's valuable cup was stolen. The neighbour consulted Harry Pot who, through 'sorcery', named Cristina as the thief. The scandalised Freemans protested innocence, and Pot confessed to being a con man who had used the same trick many times. He was sentenced to the pillory, though only for an hour.

LOVE AND SEX

Noble marriages were usually arranged. Like all families with land, the Pastons of Norfolk (whose letters are a rich source of information about medieval life) wanted marriages that increased their wealth and social status. So John Paston (1421–66) was put out when his daughter Margery declared her love for Richard Calle, the family bailiff. There were no doubt family rows and even threats, but Margery held out and married Calle anyway.

ABELARD AND HELOISE

Of true-love matches none ended more disastrously than the story of Abelard and Heloise. French theologian Peter Abelard fell in love with his young and brilliant pupil Heloise. There was a child and a secret marriage, but Heloise's uncle, Canon Fulbert, was scandalised. Perhaps having designs on Heloise himself, he had Abelard attacked by two thugs, who castrated him. The lovers were separated, Abelard becoming a monk and Heloise a nun, but their love remained. He died in 1142, she in 1163. The thugs got their just desserts: they suffered the same fate as Abelard and were blinded, and the uncle was dismissed from his position at Notre Dame Cathedral.

◄ Medieval lovers Abelard and Heloise.

➤ The first marriage of Lucrezia Borgia, the illegitimate daughter of Rodrigo Borgia.

MARRIAGE LINES

The Church rule was that girls should not marry before the age of 12 and boys not before 14, but royal couples were often betrothed (promised in marriage) long before puberty. Girls were often judged ready for the marriage bed after their first period. In 1493, Italian heiress Lucrezia Borgia was married aged 13, but the union was annulled when she was 17. Her second husband was murdered by her brother Cesare – with whom Borgia enemies said she had committed incest. The Borgias were hardly an everyday medieval family, but many families had marital secrets best kept hidden. Divorce was forbidden, except on exceptional grounds, such as non-consummation.

FIRST NIGHT RIGHTS

The 'droit du seigneur' (the right of a feudal lord to have sex with any woman under his lordship, including newlyweds) is not supported by historical evidence; although it is likely some barons abused their power, as did others. Poor peasant girls were fair game and had few means of redress against sexual exploitation.

SEX MATTERS

To enjoy sex could be scandalous in itself, since for a man to have sex for pleasure alone was to treat his wife as a whore. However, prostitution was tolerated. Medieval street names often gave away their trade (Fish, Bread, Poultry, and so on) and sex was no different. Grape or Grove Street may once have been 'Grope', and Cocks Lane needs little explanation.

Christian married couples were barred from sex on Sundays, holy feast days, and when the woman was menstruating, pregnant or breast-feeding. In Boccaccio's Decameron tales of the mid-1300s, an older husband deals with the exhausting demands of a young wife by finding so many 'no-sex days' in the calendar that she is limited to sex once a month. While foreplay was permissible (arousing the woman's body-heat was believed to aid conception), the Church frowned on sexual gymnastics, oral sex and same-sex unions. Since adultery was a sin, Queen Isabella of France (and wife of King Edward II) had morality on her side, if not family loyalty, when she became suspicious of her sisters-in-law.

THE PARIS TOWER SCANDAL

Queen Isabella was the daughter of King Philip IV of France, and her three brothers had all made political marriages. On a trip home in 1313, Isabella gave purses to her sisters-in-law, but when they visited England the purses were being flourished by two escort knights. She told her father, and spies reported that two royal sisters-in-law were having drink-fuelled romps with the knights in an old tower, liaisons of which the third wife was aware. The king had the knights tortured and executed in gruesome fashion, and the adulterous wives were publicly shamed then imprisoned. Having done her moral duty, Isabella went on to commit the very same offence years later with Roger Mortimer.

FAIR ROSAMUND

Rosamund Clifford, daughter of a Marcher baron in Herefordshire, probably met King Henry II in 1163 on his way to fight the Welsh. They became lovers in about 1166, when Queen Eleanor of Aquitaine was pregnant. Eleanor was understandably miffed and refused to have her baby (the future King John) at Woodstock, after hearing that Henry had installed 'fair Rosamund' there. Rosamund eventually retired to a nunnery; after her death it was whispered that she had been poisoned by Queen Eleanor. This seems highly unlikely, though the Bishop of Lincoln had Rosamund's tomb moved after it attracted too many visitors.

◄ Fair Rosamund Clifford and Queen Eleanor of Aquitaine, painted by Edward Burne-Jones.

WIFE-BEATING

A husband was permitted to beat his wife, but only when sober. He was forbidden to use violence against her in anger. A woman who abused her neighbours or spread scandal might be called a 'scold' and forced to wear a bridle to hold her tongue.

THE CRUELLEST CUT

In the reign of Henry II, Norfolk knight Godfrey de Millers lusted after the daughter of a fellow knight and so arranged a tryst. However, she told her father and when Godfrey arrived at her bedroom, he was set upon, beaten, suspended from a beam and 'disgracefully mutilated'. The over-zealous father was banished and the king ordered that mutilation for fornication was unlawful – except for adultery with a man's wife.

◄ Success in the lists could mean a knight caught a lady's eye.

▼ A royal wedding was not always followed by marital harmony.

THE TEMPLAR SCANDAL

The sudden and scandalous fall of the Knights Templar in the 1300s left a legacy of mystery that still fascinates conspiracy theorists. A French knight led the first Templars in 1119, their mission to win back Jerusalem for Christendom and protect pilgrims to the Holy Land. Templar knights took a vow of chastity, but their campaigns, plus perks such as tax-exemptions, helped them to grow rich (they bought Cyprus, for example), and as honest bankers their reputation stood high among Muslims and Christians. Henry II granted the Templars lands in England, where they built churches, including the Temple Church in London. In 1214 King John took refuge there during his dispute with his barons; prominent in negotiations at this time was William Marshal, Earl of Pembroke, the most famous knight of the age. Shortly before his death he became a Templar and was buried in the Temple Church.

END OF THE TEMPLARS

In the late 1200s Muslim armies overran the Christian kingdoms in the Holy Land and the Templars fought bravely to defend them. Yet in Europe their power, wealth and secrecy aroused envy and suspicion. The Templars' fall was catastrophic and sudden. On Friday 13 October 1307, every Templar in France was arrested by King Philip IV, greedy for Templar money. He gave credence to the most scandalous allegations: that initiates spat on the crucifix and took part in blasphemous ceremonies with idols; and that Templars encouraged sodomy and had secret treaties with Muslim rulers. Under torture, Templars confessed, even the Grand Master Jacques de Molay.

Pope Clement V's own interrogators cast doubt on these lurid allegations, and Edward II of

▲ The Templars' church, Temple Church in London.

▲ At the Council of Vienne in France (1312), the Church withdrew papal support from the Templars. King Philip of France got his way.

◀ Jacques de Molay, last Grand Master of the Knights Templar.

▲ Templars about to be burned as heretics, at the instigation of the French king.

TEMPLAR SECRETS

The Templars were said to guard the secrets of the Holy Grail and the genealogy of Jesus. The Grail, the cup used at the Last Supper, was said to have been brought to Britain by Joseph of Arimathea, and in legend was sought by King Arthur's knights. Even more startling is the suggestion that the Templars knew about and protected the blood-line of Jesus: a rich stimulus for fertile imaginations.

England asked for more evidence, but in France the Templars were doomed. In May 1310, fifty-four were burned to death as heretics, and in 1312 the Pope dissolved the Order, transferring all Templar property to the Knights Hospitallers. Jacques de Molay was burned at the stake in 1314. In England, Templars were imprisoned, but others fled by land and sea. Fantasists speculate that a Templar may have reached America; others believe they sailed to Scotland and rode into battle at Bannockburn to help Robert the Bruce. From the fog of myth enveloping the Templars have emerged many books and films. Though short on evidence, their possible fate makes for an engrossing story.

COURT POLITICS

Edward II, King of England in 1307, raised eyebrows. His fondness for ditch-digging and wall-building was un-lordly; keeping strange animals such as camels was eccentric; his love of hunting was not matched with skill as a soldier. Most suspect was his 'unnatural' affection for Piers Gaveston, a Gascon knight adept at jousting and delivering colourful insults. There is little evidence for a homosexual relationship, but rumour bubbled, and civil war even threatened until disgruntled barons had Gaveston beheaded in June 1312.

The Despensers

Only one baron, Hugh Despenser, supported Gaveston, and thus earned Edward's favour. Despenser got rich, his son (also Hugh) supplementing the family income from Channel piracy. The Despensers saw off rivals like Thomas of Lancaster (executed in 1322) and thrived until Queen Isabella, their arch-enemy, landed with an army from France in 1326 to remove them. Both were executed as traitors; the younger Despenser suffering the full horrors of medieval execution: part-hanged, revived, and his body quartered, his sexual organs were cut off and thrown into a fire, followed by his entrails. His agonies were watched by a large crowd that included the queen.

Did Edward II die?

Isabella, the 'She-Wolf of France', was cheered for removing the Despensers. Despising her husband, Edward II, she had taken a baron-lover called Roger

▲ Piers Gaveston's head is presented to the barons who brought him down. In the centre is Thomas, Earl of Lancaster, and with him are the earls of Hereford and Arundel.

▲ Berkeley Castle, Gloucestershire, where Edward II was held prisoner and probably killed.

Mortimer and in 1327 they staged a coup. The Bishop of Hereford openly declared the king a sodomite and tyrant, and Mortimer called on Parliament to depose Edward. The king was held at Kenilworth Castle, forced to abdicate, and then moved to Berkeley Castle, where it is generally assumed he died. His son, now Edward III, was told so in September 1327, and various accounts seeped out: illness; a fall; starvation; smothering; strangulation. The most lurid story was that Edward was killed by the anal insertion of a red-hot iron. A royal body lay in state for two months, but so covered that none could swear as to the identity of the corpse. Later, some even suggested the king had escaped – a letter found in the 1870s was proposed as 'proof' and held that Edward II went to live in Italy.

ALICE PERRERS

When Edward III reached his later years he became besotted with Alice Perrers. The daughter of a tiler or a weaver, according to scandal-mongers, Alice was more likely of noble birth, since she was a lady-in-waiting to Queen Philippa. Edward gave Alice some of the late queen's jewels, which Alice showed off shamelessly, riding through London in 1375 dressed as 'The Lady of the Sun' to attend a tournament. In 1377 she encouraged, perhaps cruelly, the ailing King Edward to go hunting, and when he collapsed and died she made off with his rings.

FAIR MAID'S MARRIAGES

Joan, the Fair Maid of Kent, was said to be the most beautiful woman in England. She was first married in 1341 (aged 13) to William Montacute, son of the Earl of Salisbury. Six years later, Thomas Holland, home from the Crusades, insisted Joan and he had married secretly in 1340. The reportedly bigamous Joan was locked up by her irate father-in-law, but in 1349 the Pope declared her Montacute marriage annulled and she was restored to Holland, bearing four children. After Holland died, Joan married the king's heir, the Black Prince, and in 1367 at Bordeaux bore a son. The baby, said to be born skinless, had to be swaddled in goatskin. In 1377 he became King Richard II.

▼ In his pomp, Edward III challenges Philip VI of France, whose realm he claimed.

POLL TAX REVOLT

The Peasants' Revolt of 1381 was sparked by resentment over taxation and, in particular, the poll tax levied on every person in a household over 14. To avoid the tax, many people 'disappeared', leading taxmen to wonder how England's population had shrunk by almost one-third! It had in fact shrunk by almost this much after the Black Death plague of 1348–50. In 1381, however, peaceful protest turned violent: radical Lollards joined in and the rebels executed the Archbishop of Canterbury and the royal treasurer, and looted John of Gaunt's palace. One impudent 'peasant' (so the story went) demanded a kiss from the Fair Maid Joan, who fainted.

USURPER AND CONQUEROR

Richard II's reign ended in 1399 with his overthrow by Henry of Lancaster, who became Henry IV. Henry never sat easily on the throne, and to some

▲ Richard II, King of England from 1377–99.

the punishment for his usurpation was visually evident – Henry suffered a 'rotting of the flesh, a drying-up of the eyes, and a rupture of the intestines'. He also had a head-louse problem.

The king lived in fear of assassination. Uprisings in Wales were led by Owen Glyndwr. And equally troublesome, especially in Shakespeare's version of events written later, was his own son Prince Hal, who after a rowdy, even dissolute youth in the London taverns metamorphoses into Henry V, victor at Agincourt. Henry V had a ruthless streak that might have been enough to secure his ambition – to rule both France and England – except he succumbed to dysentery in 1422, leaving an infant son, Henry VI, and plunging England into a dynastic bloodbath.

▲ The peasants, led by Wat Tyler, burn the Palace of the Savoy in 1381 (painted by Alfred Garth Jones, 1900).

BAD OMENS

Richard II's coronation was beset by bad omens. One of his shoes came off, as did a spur; worst of all, at the banquet the wind blew off his crown, presaging his overthrow. Richard was accused of extravagance by his enemies, with hundreds of hangers-on being fed daily, everyone overdressed, and there was a constant search for new fashions.

CIVIL WAR SECRETS

enry VI remained in the care of his relatives, principally the Duke of York, until 1437. He was religious, reclusive and easily shocked. He walked out of a Christmas entertainment at which topless dancers cavorted, and was scandalised by the sight of naked men taking the waters at Bath. Reportedly ever-watchful for 'any foolish impertinence of women', the king suffered bouts of 'madness', lost all his father's conquests in France, and became a helpless pawn in the bloody Wars of the Roses between the Lancaster and York factions. During poor Henry's reign he was captured, rescued, deposed, recaptured, imprisoned, reinstated and then murdered in 1471. Mocked in life, he was posthumously venerated as a saint.

EDWARD OF YORK

Edward IV was helped to the throne in 1461 by the fickle Earl of Warwick (later called 'the Kingmaker'). Edward was a good soldier, but a French

▲ Edward IV, civil war victor sapped by 'debauchery'.

◄ The coronation of the boy-king Henry VI.

commentator noted he 'thought upon nothing but women' when not on the battlefield. In 1464 Edward married Elizabeth Woodville in secret, aware that her greedy relatives were ambitious and she was disliked by his friends. The Woodville connection so angered Warwick that the Kingmaker deserted Edward and helped restore Henry VI, albeit briefly.

Despite his own womanising, Edward IV ruled reasonably well, with his clinically efficient brother Richard of Gloucester at his side. Their younger brother, Clarence, had sided with Warwick during his revolt and was untrustworthy ever after; in 1478 he was 'removed', apparently drowned in a butt of wine. Richard looked after northern England, while Edward grew fat, enjoying the charms of his mistress Elizabeth ('Jane') Shore. The king died, 'worn out by debaucheries', in 1483, and the fates of his two sons became one of the abiding mysteries of English history.

the Crown. In 1485 Henry defeated Richard III at the Battle of Bosworth and became Henry VII, the first Tudor king. The fate of the vanished princes sparked speculation for succeeding generations.

BONES IN A STAIRWAY

In 1674 workmen found 'small bones' beneath a Tower stairway, which were reburied in Westminster Abbey on the assumption that they were the two princes. Experts examined the bones in 1933 and confirmed their identity, although this verdict has been questioned. One possible clue comes from Anne Mowbray, daughter of the Duke of Norfolk, who died in 1481 aged 8. Her coffin and skeleton were found in 1965, and forensic evidence suggests both sets of bones are related: Anne and the princes had common great-grandparents. DNA testing on the Westminster Abbey bones has so far been refused by Abbey authorities.

▼ Richard III at the Battle of Bosworth.

▲ Edward V (1470–83?) and Richard of York (1473–83?), as often portrayed: the tragic 'Princes in the Tower'.

RICHARD AND THE PRINCES

As soon as Edward IV was buried, Richard of Gloucester took the uncrowned king, Edward V, and his brother Prince Richard into his 'protection'. The Woodville marriage was declared illegal, making the princes bastards, and Richard III was duly crowned on 6 July 1483. The two boys disappeared into the Tower of London. They were briefly seen in the garden and at windows, but had almost certainly been murdered by September. Stories spread that one or both had survived with new identities, and 'pretenders' were later to appear.

Richard III remains a prime suspect for the murders. Yet others also had motives. Margaret Beaufort, the ambitious mother of Henry Tudor, was keen to eliminate York rivals as her son prepared his bid for

NORTh OF The BORDER

Things were no less violent in Scotland in the 1400s, mainly due to a succession of juvenile kings. James I, kidnapped as a boy by English pirates, was held prisoner in England for eighteen years while Scotland was ruled by Governor Albany, and then his incompetent son Murdoch. Following the payment of a ransom, James returned, but was murdered in 1437. His son became James II at the age of 6.

James II met an unlikely end in 1460 when, supporting Henry VI during the Wars of the Roses, he was blown up by one of his own cannon at the siege of Roxburgh Castle.

His son James III was not yet 10 when crowned. His was a troubled reign, for his brothers Albany and Mar conspired against him. Mar died suspiciously, while Albany escaped to England to claim recognition as King Alexander IV. James's unorthodox sexuality so alarmed the court that

▲ James IV, King of Scotland (r.1488–1513).

scandalised lords hanged one of his boyfriends. They then tried to promote the king's 15-year-old son, James. Father and son fought at Sauchieburn in 1488 and James III was killed. A penitent James IV married the daughter of Henry VII of England, but a rash invasion across the border in 1513 led to his death at Flodden – a tragic finale to a typically medieval chronicle of scandalous misadventure.

REPUTATION SULLIED

Just like today, medieval whistle-blowers could face character assassination. In 1479, after a row during which Thomas Norton accused the Mayor of Bristol of treason, Norton's reputation was attacked by the city council. They told King Edward IV that Norton was 'a common haunter of taverns', he lay in bed until nine or ten o'clock, and instead of church preferred tennis and 'other such frivolous disports'. The king dismissed the treason charge.

PLACES TO VISIT

The United Kingdom has a rich medieval heritage, with sites and heritage centres across England, Wales, Scotland and Northern Ireland. There is much to interest and delight, and to make the spine tingle and the flesh creep. Some properties are in public ownership; others are privately owned, but most are open to the public for at least some days in the year. There is space here to mention only a selection of places to visit for a taste of medieval life, and the secrets and scandals that were part of its rich tapestry.

▲ Hever Castle.

Battle Abbey and 1066 Battlefield
High St, Battle, East Sussex, TN33 0AD
www.english-heritage.org.uk/battleabbey

Colchester Castle
Castle Park, Colchester, Essex, CO1 1TJ
www.colchestermuseums.org.uk and follow the link

Dover Castle
Castle Hill, Dover, Kent, CT16 1HU
www.english-heritage.org.uk/daysout/properties/dover-castle/

Durham Castle
Palace Green, Durham, DH1 3RW
Entry by guided tour only; www.dur.ac.uk/university.college

Hever Castle
Hever Road, Hever, Kent, TN8 7NG
www.hevercastle.co.uk

Imperial War Museum
IWM London, Lambeth Road, London, SE1 6HZ
www.iwm.org.uk/visits/iwm-london

Imperial War Museum North
The Quays, Trafford Wharf Road,
Manchester, M17 1TZ
www.iwm.org.uk/visits/iwm-north

Kenilworth Castle
Castle Green, Kenilworth, Warwickshire,
CV8 1NE
www.english-heritage.org.uk/Kenilworth

National Maritime Museum
Park Row, Greenwich, London, SE10 9NF
www.rmg.co.uk/maritimemuseum

National War Museum of Scotland
Edinburgh Castle, Castlehill, Edinburgh,
Midlothian, EH1 2NG
www.nms.ac.uk/our_museums/war_
museum.aspx

Nottingham Castle
Castle Place, Nottingham, NG1 6EL
www.nottinghamcity.gov.uk/Castle

Palace of Holyroodhouse
Edinburgh, EH8 8DX
www.royalcollection.org.uk

Richmond Castle
Riverside Road, Richmond, North Yorkshire, DL10 4QW
www.english-heritage.org.uk/daysout/properties/richmond-castle

Royal Armouries, HM Tower of London
London, EC3N 4AB
www.royalarmouries.org/tower-of-london

Royal Armouries Museum, Leeds
Armouries Drive, Leeds, LS10 1LT
www.royalarmouries.org/leeds

Runnymede
Surrey, SL4 2JL
www.nationaltrust.org.uk/runnymede

Tower of London
London, EC3N 4AB
www.hrp.org.uk/TowerOfLondon

Warwick Castle
Warwick, Warwickshire, CV34 4QU
www.warwick-castle.co.uk

Windsor Castle
Windsor, Berkshire, SL4 1NJ
www.royalcollection.org.uk/visit/
windsorcastle

◄ Magna Carta Memorial at Runnymede, Surrey. The memorial was created by the American Bar Association in 1957.